Pebble® Plus

Dogs, Dogs, Dogs

All about Boxers

by Erika L. Shores

Consulting Editor: Gail Saunders-Smith, PhD

CAPSTONE PRESS
a capstone imprint

Pebble Plus is published by Capstone Press,
1710 Roe Crest Drive, North Mankato, Minnesota 56003.
www.capstonepub.com

Library of Congress Cataloging-in-Publication Data
Shores, Erika L., 1976–
All about boxers / by Erika L. Shores.
p. cm.—(Pebble plus. dogs, dogs, dogs)
Summary: "Full-color photographs and simple text provide a brief introduction to boxers"—Provided by publisher.
ISBN 978-1-4296-8723-2 (library binding)
ISBN 978-1-62065-291-6 (ebook PDF)
1. Boxer (Dog breed)—Juvenile literature. I. Title.
SF429.B75S46 2013
636.73—dc23   2011049816

Editorial Credits
Veronica Correia, designer; Marcie Spence, media researcher; Kathy McColley, production specialist

Photo Credits
Capstone Studio: Karon Dubke, 5; Fiona Green Animal Photography: 1, 3, 9, 11, 17, 19, 21; Shutterstock: cynoclub, 15,
Jeff Thrower, cover, SueC, 13, Whytock, 7

Note to Parents and Teachers

The Dogs, Dogs, Dogs series supports national science standards related to life science. This
book describes and illustrates boxers. The images support early readers in understanding the
text. The repetition of words and phrases helps early readers learn new words. This book
also introduces early readers to subject-specific vocabulary words, which are defined in the
Glossary section. Early readers may need assistance to read some words and to use the Table of
Contents, Glossary, Read More, Internet Sites, and Index sections of the book.

Printed in the United States of America in North Mankato, Minnesota.
042012   006682CGF12

Table of Contents

Family Dogs

Boxers like to be around kids
more than almost
any other dog breed.
Boxers are loyal and
loving family pets.

Boxers are brave and
make good guard dogs.
They will stand between
a family member
and a stranger.

The Boxer Look

Boxers are medium-sized dogs. They stand 21 to 25 inches (53 to 64 centimeters) tall at the withers. The tops of an animal's shoulders are called the withers.

Boxers have wrinkly heads.
Long wrinkles are on either side
of the muzzle. When a boxer's
ears stick up, many wrinkles
show up on its forehead.

A boxer's short coat is fawn

or brindle with white markings.

Fawn is light tan to red-brown.

Brindle is black or fawn stripes

on a solid coat.

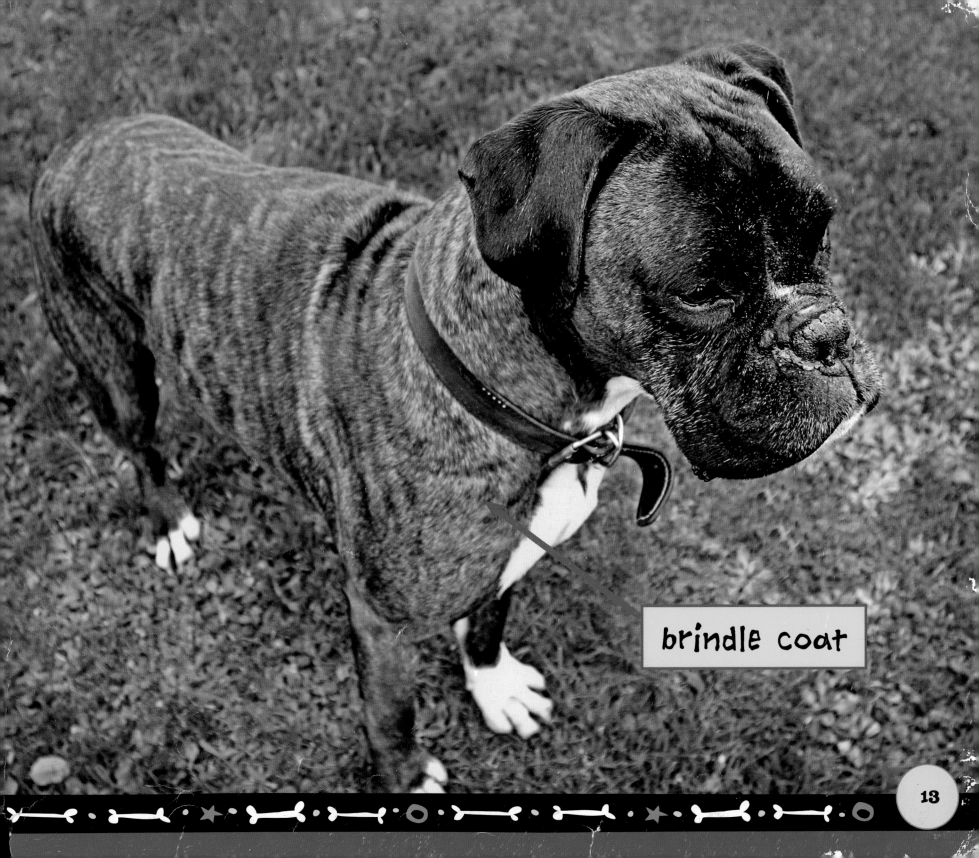

brindle coat

Puppy Time

A female boxer gives birth

to five to 10 puppies in a litter.

The wrinkly puppies grow quickly.

Healthy boxers live between

eight and 10 years.

Doggie Duties

Boxers lick their coats

to stay clean like cats do.

Boxers don't often need baths.

But they do shed. Owners

should brush them weekly.

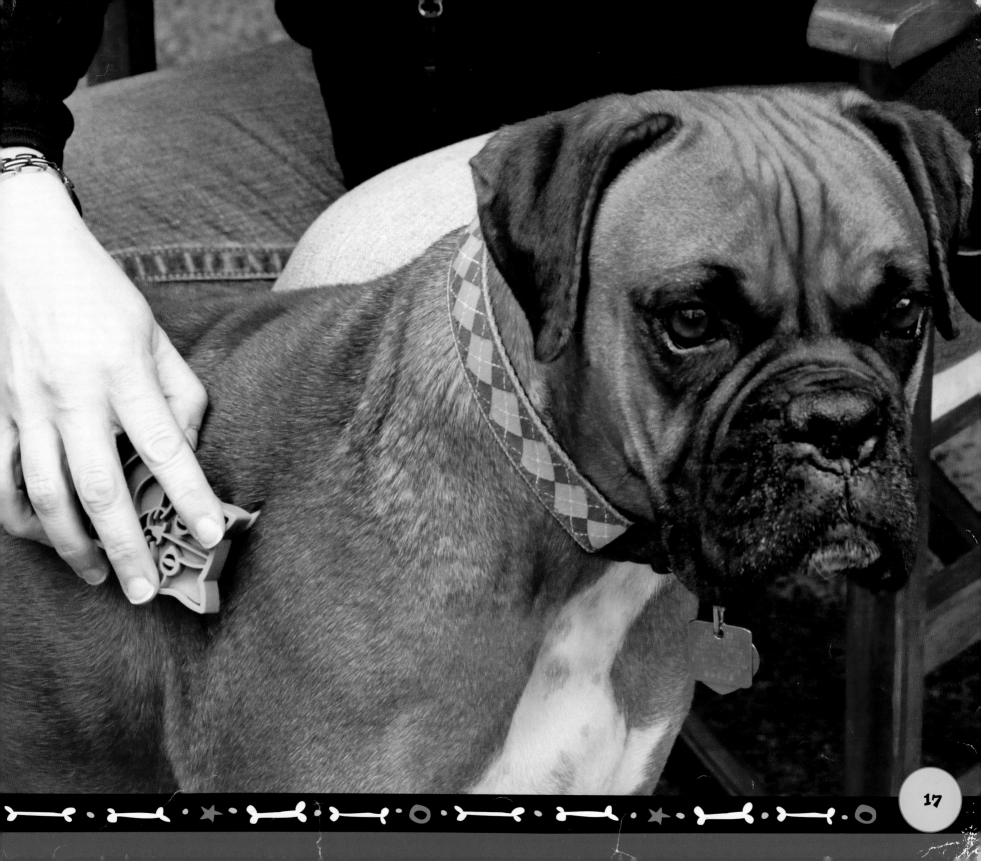

Boxers are active dogs.
Owners should make sure
boxers get plenty of exercise.
At least two walks a day
will keep a boxer happy.

Bouncing Boxers

Playful boxers bounce around.

They move their feet like

a person boxing in a ring.

The dogs then leap into the air

to catch balls or flying discs.

Glossary

active—being busy and moving around

brave—having courage

breed—a certain kind of animal within an animal group

brindle—a solid coat color mixed with black or fawn stripes

coat—an animal's hair or fur

fawn—a light tan to red-brown color

loyal—being true to something or someone

markings—patches of color on fur

muzzle—an animal's nose, mouth, and jaws

shed—to lose hair

withers—the tops of an animal's shoulders; a dog's height is measured from the ground to the withers

Read More

Green, Sara. *Boxers.* Dog Breeds. Minneapolis: Bellwether Media, 2009.

Hanson, Anders. *Bold Boxers.* Dog Daze. Edina, Minn.: ABDO, 2009.

Johnson, J. Angelique. *Getting a Pet: Step-by-Step.* Step-by-Step Stories. Mankato, Minn.: Capstone Press, 2012.

Internet Sites

FactHound offers a safe, fun way to find Internet sites related to this book. All of the sites on FactHound have been researched by our staff.

Here's all you do:

Visit *www.facthound.com*

Type in this code: 9781429687232

 Check out projects, games and lots more at **www.capstonekids.com**

Index

Word Count: 221
Grade: 1
Early-Intervention Level: 16